Also by the Author

The Ghost Engine

She thought she could change the world…

When Lady Elizabeth Ada Lovelace, a beautiful, arrogant suffragette, purchased the 19th-century Algorithmic Engine in order to become the world's first programmer, she planned to break the shackles of inequality for Victorian women.

Until her world became that of the machine…

Instead she learns the true meaning of equality when she ends up trapped, brought down to the level of the machine. Inside the double-crossing computer, Elizabeth must match wits with a stubbornly idealistic ghost and a chillingly handsome doppelganger in the computer's endless series of mind games. But as the machine learns to become a sentient being, time is ticking away. Elizabeth finds herself falling in love with the ghost trapped in the machine. Together they are pitted in a race against the machine to escape before the Algorithmic Engine shuts down – killing them all.

Now all their worlds hang in the balance.

The Girl Who Became a Goddess

The Girl Who Became a Goddess is a tribute to the childhood stories of Theresa Fuller who has experienced multiple cultures and learned to love them all. These are tales passed on from generation to generation, some to delight, some to terrify, all to enlighten.

> *A foolish animal discovers that the Rainforest is a dangerous place.*
> *A young boy is willing to sacrifice everything for his family.*
> *A woman must decide between the man she loves and the human race.*

As a girl, a mother, and a teacher, Theresa retells her favorite folktales through the lens of her own life experiences in Singapore, Malaysia and Australia, putting a unique spin on ageless classics.

The Girl Who Became a Goddess is a love letter to a young girl from the adult she has become.

The Girl Sudan Painted Like a Gold Ring

If you like your fables with a dash of bloodshed, then *The Girl Sudan Painted Like a Gold Ring* is the anthology you have been waiting for. Author Theresa Fuller has collected a fascinating group of tales based on the oral storytelling history of the Sea Dyaks of Borneo. The twist? The Dyaks were headhunters!

A tiny mousedeer battles a spirit giant
A girl must save her village from an army of head-hunters
How a hedgehog helps a bullied boy become a god

In this book you will find stories designed to entertain and teach, all from the point of view of a culture based in honor, courtesy, and war.

The Baba Malay Today Series

Baba Malay - the language of the Peranakans is about to go extinct, but you can reverse the process by learning Baba Malay in clearly defined steps. This treasured language can be a part of your life, hopefully to be revived as it is spread through sharing this didactic method.

Former assessor and examiner of the Higher School Certificate (NSW, Australia), Theresa Fuller, known fondly in the Peranakan community as Bibek Theresa, draws on her years of experience in the classroom to create the Baba Malay Today series – a range of chapter books with an easy-to-follow curriculum aimed at the beginner.

Books 1 & 2 – Interrogatory
Sapa, Apa, Mana or Who, What, Where
Amcham, Apasair, Bila or How, What, When
Book 3 – Conjunctions
Tapi, Abis, Pasair or But, So, Because
Book 4 – Prepositions
Atair, Kat, Bawah or Top, Near, Bottom
Book 5 – Antonyms
Alus, Ka, Kasar or Delicate, Or, Coarse

THERESA FULLER

Where Cranes Weave And Bamboo Sings

The Write Start: A Visual Narrative Workbook for Teachers and Writers

Bare Bear Media

© Theresa Fuller 2023
All Rights Reserved.

No part of this publication may be reproduced, stored in a retrieval system, or transmitted, in any form or by any means electronic, mechanical, photocopying, recording or otherwise, without the prior written permission of the publishers.

Theresa Fuller asserts the moral right to be identified as the author of this work.
Bare Bear Media

ISBN 978-1-925748-14-7

ISBN 978-1-925748-15-4

Editors
Karen Albright Lin
Dayna Hart

Design and Illustration
Peggy Sands, Indigo Disegno

Copyright
National Library of Australia
US Library of Congress - TXu 2-364-065
Published 31st March 2023

Dedicated to

*To my husband, Paul, who supported this work
in every way possible. I love you.*

*To Jonathan, if it wasn't for you and homeschooling
because of the Covid lockdown, this book
would not have been born.*

*To Tim, the best editor in the business.
Thank you for your tireless checking.*

TABLE OF CONTENTS

Foreword	11	Remember – The Hero always has a Goal	42
Introduction	13	Now you try	43
Epigraph	14	*Grace Darling*	44
Notes to Teachers – On how to start	15	*The Flute*	46
The Basics	16	*The Ugly Duckling*	48
Putting It All Together	26	Consolidation of the Beginning	50
Mind Map 1 (Simple)	29	Notes to Teachers – On Polishing	53
Now it's Your Turn	31	Unedited Version of Sally's Birthday	54
Noah	32	Edited Version of Sally's Birthday	55
Sang Kancil	34	Introducing Call to Adventure	56
The Dutch Boy who Saved the Dike	36	Notes to Teachers – Call to Adventure	58
Consolidation of the Basics	38	*King Solomon and the Baby*	60
Introducing When, Where and Why	40	Introducing Change of Plans	62

The Middle	63
Now you try (Find the change of plans)	65
The Three Little Pigs	66
Nukhudu	70
Notes to Teachers – Tragedy	75
The Gingerbread Man	76
Notes to Teachers – More on Tragedy	80
The Crane Wife	82
Consolidation of the Beginning, & Middle	86
Introducing The Climax	88
The Resolution	89
Introducing The Antagonist	90
Now you try. Find the Antagonist.	93
The Old Man of the Sea	94
Hansel and Gretel	98
Notes to Teachers – the Hero	102
Now you try	105
The ORIGINAL Little Mermaid	106
Puteri Gunung Ledang	112
The Weeping Lady	116
Consolidation of Narrative	122
Mind Map 2 (Advanced)	124
Now it's Your Turn	125
About the Author	127
Acknowledgements	129

FOREWORD

I first knew Theresa Fuller as a student in one of my synopses writing classes. From the start Theresa impressed me – she was the only student to complete all the homework. This was no mean feat. As most writers know, the synopsis is often the bane of a writer's tasks, many often leaving it to the last. Or omitting it completely.

So it was with great delight to learn that not only had she completed the work I had set, but in the process enjoyed it tremendously.

While others were tearing their hair out, she was having fun!

Since that first day, Theresa has taken more of my classes and our relationship has grown to one of mutual friendship as we discover that we share many things in common.

With a degree in computing, a master's degree in Education, and years spent honing her writing skills by producing books on folktales, it makes sense that if anyone was to take on the task of deconstructing narrative into its constituent parts that it would be Theresa. She has used her systems analysis training to pinpoint the necessary components in story – an ability that many writers struggle with, and her teaching skills to create an easy-to-follow curriculum.

Combined with her experience as a former HSC examiner and assessor for the New South Wales Board of Studies, I strongly believe that Theresa has produced an excellent study guide on narrative suitable for students as well as the novice writer.

As Theresa was originally from Southeast Asia, I have encouraged her to share the tales that she grew up with. So not only has she produced a text on narrative but one that illuminates the seldom told stories of an often-forgotten part of the world.

~ Karen Albright Lin, Author of *Mu Shu Mac and Cheese, American Moon, A Chinese Immigration Story*

INTRODUCTION

Writing and story-telling is thousands of years old, from simple cave painting diagrams to the oral traditions of bards singing epic poems to their audience. Then on to more complex systems that developed into manuscripts, and hand printed books which later evolved when the first printing press was invented. No matter the medium, there are writers who create characters and worlds to entertain, to instruct and to influence. The digital age allows fast dissemination of words and stories in a new medium. Theresa Fuller's workbook inspires with its simple explanations, diagrams and illustrations. It is an easy-to-read and use reference material for teachers and students, or the writer learning alone. Theresa's passion for writing and teaching clearly shows in the presentation of this workbook and it will surely inspire a new generation of writers to weave their tales in unique ways to a new audience.

"I kept always two books in my pocket, one to read, one to write in."

~Robert Louis Stevenson

"I die unless I write." ~ *Theresa Fuller*

Notes to Teachers

For many writers knowing where to begin a story is difficult.

Trying to write a textbook for the different stages of learning is equally so. Consequently, I have divided the book into 2 parts, but this is simply a suggestion.

You know your students best.

1. Pages 1 to 38 for ages 5 to 12.

2. Ages 13 and older may proceed from the start and work their way through. I wrote this resource for beginning writers whatever their age.

Again, I stress there are as many ways to teach writing as there are to write. There are no absolutes in writing. It has been a dilemma deciding what to include or exclude.

All pages except Notes to Teachers may be reproduced onto slides, hence the larger font size.

The Three Part Structure is probably the most popular, but there are many more. As I say to my students: do what works for you. This book is simply a guide. Learn the basics, then experiment to find your own style and voice.
At the end of the day, have fun with your writing.

If you have found this workbook helpful, then please drop me a line.

Theresa Fuller
Sydney
6th of July 2022

www.theresafuller.com

P.O. Box 7021
Mt Annan
NSW, 2567
Australia

The Basics

A narrative tells a story.

A story has **3** parts.

Beginning

Middle

End

Beginning

Who A narrative starts with a person or a thing – (**Hero**)
What they want – (**Goal**)
Which thing stops them from getting it – (**Conflict**)

Example:

Sally wanted **a cake** for her birthday, but there was **no flour** in the cupboard.

The middle of the story shows how the character tries to solve the problem. **How** they try to get their goal.

EXAMPLE:

Sally **went to the shops**. She **bought flour**. Then she came home and **made the cake**.

End

The end is how the problem is solved or fixed. **Resolution**.

Example:
Everyone sang. Then **Sally cut the cake**. Everyone had a slice.

PUTTING IT ALL TOGETHER:

Sally wanted **a cake** for her birthday, but there was **no flour** in the cupboard.

So Sally **went to the shops**. She **bought flour**. Then she came home and **made the cake.**

Everyone sang. Then **Sally cut the cake**. Everyone had a slice.

A narrative tells a story.
A story is a description of
actual or *fictional* events.

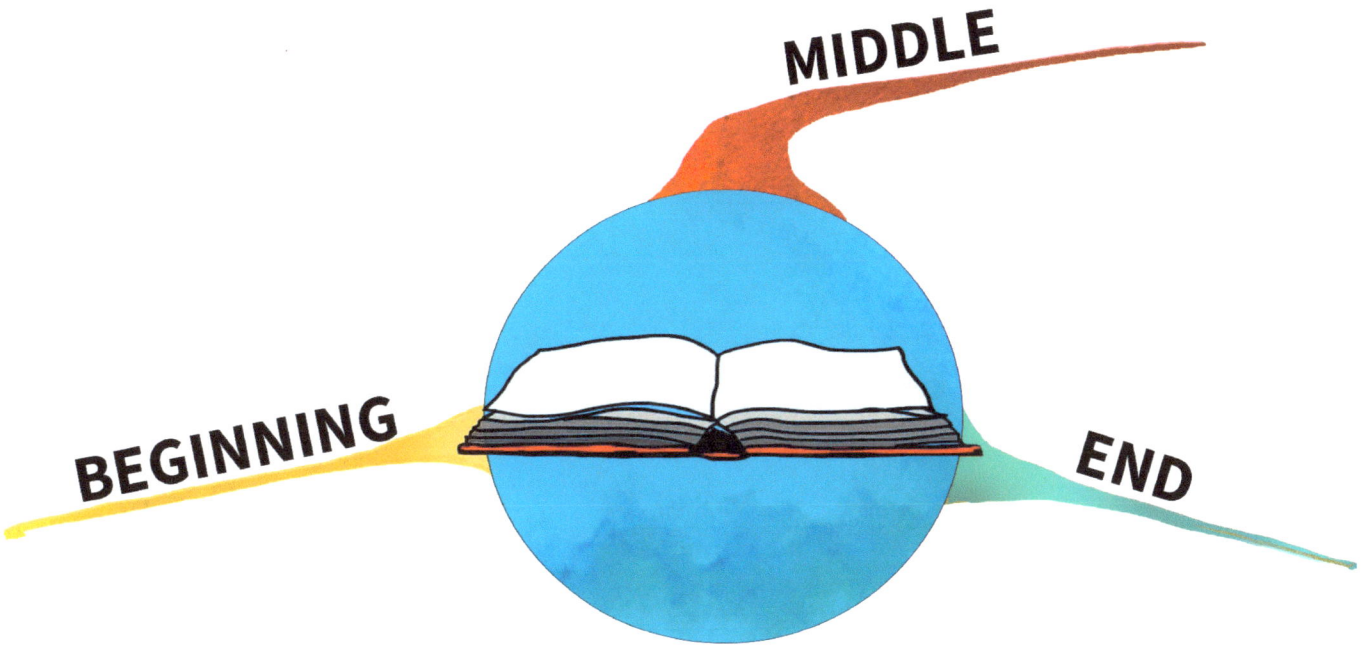

Mind Map (Simple)

A story has 3 main parts.

Now it's *your* turn.

NOAH

Noah was a good man. Noah learned God was sending **a flood** that would destroy everything, but Noah wanted to **keep his family safe**.

Noah **built a special boat** called an ark. He **put animals, food, and his family on the ark**.

The rain started. When the rain stopped, and the floodwater had gone down, **everyone came out, safe and sound**.

QUESTIONS

1. Who is the story about (character)?

2. What did they want (goal)?

3. What was the problem?
   (which thing stops them getting what they want?)

4. How did they solve their problem (what steps did they take)?

5. What happened in the end (was the problem fixed)?

ANSWERS

1) Noah. 2) Keep his family safe. 3) A flood. 4) Step 1 – built a boat. Step 2 – collected animals and food. 5) Yes, everyone was safe.

SANG KANCIL

Sang Kancil was a mousedeer who needed to **cross a river**, but **the river was filled with crocodiles**.

Sang Kancil **told the crocodiles that he wanted to count them** for King Solomon.

The crocodiles lined up.

Sang Kancil **leapt from back to back** as he **counted the crocodiles**.

Finally, Sang Kancil **reached the other side of the river**.

He was safe!

QUESTIONS

1. Who is the story about (character)?

2. What did he want (goal)?

3. What was the problem?
   (which thing stops him getting what he wants?)

4. How did he solve his problem (what steps did he take)?

5. What happened in the end (was the problem fixed)?

ANSWERS

1) Sang Kancil. 2) Cross a river. 3) The river was filled with crocodiles. 4) Step 1 – told the crocodiles that he wanted to count them, Step 2 – leapt from back to back, Step 3 – counted the crocodiles. 5) Yes, Sang Kancil reached the other side of the river.

THE DUTCH BOY WHO SAVED THE DIKE

In Holland, there are many dikes which prevent flooding, but one day a Dutch boy called Hans noticed a hole in a dike.

Hans knew that the hole would grow bigger, and the floodwater would threaten the village and everyone in it.

Hans plugged the hole with his finger, but the hole grew bigger. He put his whole arm into the hole, but the water was cold and the boy was afraid. He did not pull his arm out.

Hans stayed there all night, even though he was tired and cold and hungry.

QUESTIONS

1. Who is the story about (character)?

2. What did he want (goal)?

3. What was the problem (conflict)?

4. How did he solve the problem (what steps did he take)?

5. What happened in the end (was the problem fixed)?

ANSWERS

1) A little Dutch boy called Hans. 2) To stop a dike from flooding. 3) There was a hole in the dike. 4) Step 1 – plug his finger in the hole, Step 2 – place his whole arm in the hole. 5) Yes, he stood beside the dike all night to save his people, and waited until the water receded.

Consolidation *of the Basics*

A narrative is a story.
A story has **3** main parts: beginning, middle and end.

The beginning contains **who** the story is about and their name, **what** it is that they want, but **which** thing stops them.

The middle shows **how** they try to solve the problem, and **how** the problem gets worse.

The end is how the problem is solved or fixed. **Resolution**.

Introducing

When, Where and Why

THE BEGINNING

Who	the story is about	**Hero**
What	they want	**Goal**
Why	they want it	**Motivation**
Which	thing stops them	**Conflict**
When	the story takes place	**Time**
Where	it happens	**Setting**

Writing Fact

The **Who** is also called the **protagonist**.

Remember!

The **Hero** always has a
- **Goal**
- **Motivation**
- **Conflict**

Now *you* try.

GRACE DARLING

Grace Darling's father was the lighthouse keeper on **Longstone Island**. On the night of **September 7th, 1838**, **Grace** spotted survivors of a wrecked ship on a low, rocky island.

If they were not rescued **they would die**, but the storm would make it hard to reach them.

Grace and her father took a rowing boat out to rescue the survivors. While her father helped the four men and one woman onto the boat, Grace kept the boat steady.

Grace and her father got the survivors back to the lighthouse where they waited out the storm. Grace and her father were heroes!

Questions

1. Who is the story about (hero/protagonist/character)?

2. When does the story take place (time)?

3. Where does the story take place (setting)?

4. What did they want (goal)? Motivation?

5. What was the problem (conflict)?

6. How did they solve their problem (what steps did they take)?

7. What happened in the end (was the problem fixed i.e. resolution)?

Answers

1) Grace Darling. 2) September 7th, 1838. 3) Longstone Island. 4) Rescue the survivors. So they would not die. 5) There was a storm. 6) Rowed out to the island, kept the boat steady.
7) Yes, they took the survivors back to the lighthouse where they were safe.

THE FLUTE

A long time ago in **India**, there was a boy called Ali who loved to play the flute. He made such beautiful music that one day, a crocodile crawled out of the Ganges River to listen.

Ali wanted to stop, but **the crocodile threatened to eat him** if he did.

Frightened, Ali played on, but his lips ached.

He was so tired.

He stopped.

The crocodile roared!

Terrified, Ali stuck his hand out.

To his surprise, the roaring changed to a choking sound.

When Ali opened his eyes, he saw that his flute was upright, wedging open the crocodile's mouth. Ali ran away.

Questions

1. Who is the story about (hero/protagonist/character)?
2. When does the story take place (time)?
3. Where does the story take place (setting)?
4. What did he want (goal)? Motivation?
5. What was the problem (conflict)?
6. How did they solve their problem (what steps did they take)?
7. What happened in the end (was the problem fixed i.e., resolution)?

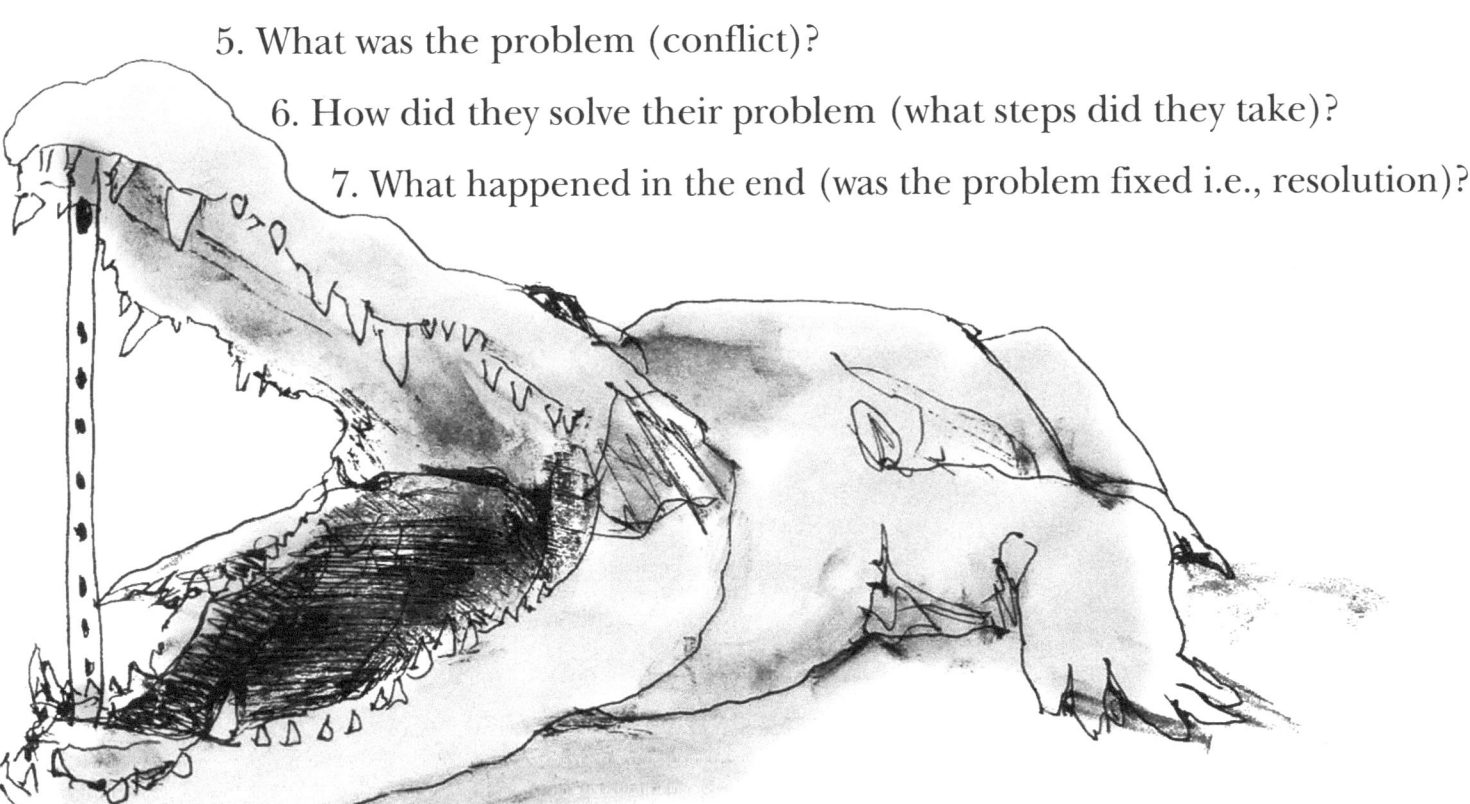

Answers

1) A boy called Ali. 2) A long time ago. 3) India. 4) To live, he did not want to die. 5) The crocodile would eat him if he stopped. 6) Jammed his flute in the mouth of the crocodile so the animal could not shut his mouth. 7) Yes, with the crocodile unable to bite, the boy could run away.

THE UGLY DUCKLING

In a farmyard, a mother duck's eggs begin to hatch.

Six fluffy ducklings emerge, quacking excitedly. They are yellow and cute.

The seventh egg hatches, and this duckling looks different from his brothers and sisters.

He is large, grey and awkward.

The seventh duckling wants to enjoy his family, but his brothers and sisters bully him.

The ugly duckling leaves home and finds shelter with an old woman and her cat, but when the cat teases the ugly duckling, he leaves.

A farmer finds the duckling and takes him in, but the duckling is afraid of the farmer's children, and he runs away again.

Finally, the duckling finds a cave, where he hides until Spring.

When Spring comes, a beautiful flock of swans arrive at the lake.

The ugly duckling approaches them, prepared for rejection, but the swans invite the ugly duckling to join them. When the duckling looks at his reflection in the water, he discovers he is not an ugly duckling, but a swan!

He flies away with his new-found family. He looks down and sees his old family far beneath him.

They are still ducks.

QUESTIONS

1. Who is the protagonist?

2. When does the story take place?

3. Where is the story set?

4. What is the goal? Motivation?

5. Conflict?

6. How did they solve their problem (what steps did they take)?

7. What happened in the end (resolution)?

ANSWERS

1) The Ugly Duckling. 2) The Ugly Duckling is a fairytale. The accepted time for when a fairytale takes place is Once upon a time. 3) The story starts off in a farmyard but any setting is appropriate for a fairytale. In this case, the story takes place in a fantasy world. 4) The duckling wanted to be loved and accepted for himself. Why? Because he was unloved. 5) The duckling did not look like the others and was considered ugly. 6) At first the duckling simply ran away but in the end, the duckling faced up to his problem. He would approach the swans even if they rejected him. 7) When he approached the swans, to his surprise, they invited him to join them. Startled, he looked down at his reflection in the water and discovered that all this time, he was not a duck but a swan.

Consolidation *of the beginning*

Narrative = story
3 main parts.
- beginning
- middle
- end

Beginning:
- hero/protagonist/character
- goal
- motivation
- conflict
- setting
- when

Middle:
- how

End:
- resolution

Notes to Teachers

Self-editing or polishing your words...

The first draft of a writer's manuscript always needs editing. A manuscript often requires various revisions to correct content — from structure, to fact check, to line editing for spelling mistakes, typos, etcetera. It is called "polishing". For example, variations in the length of sentences provide pace to the story and interest to the reader; it stops the reader from being "hypnotised" by monotonous writing.

On the next two pages are the unedited and edited versions.

UNEDITED VERSION

Sally wanted **a cake** for her birthday, but there was **no flour** in the cupboard.

So Sally **went to the shops**. She **bought flour**. Then she came home and **made the cake**.

Everyone sang. Then **Sally cut the cake**. Everyone had a slice.

EDITED VERSION

Sally wanted a cake for her birthday, but there was no flour in the cupboard.

She went to the shops and bought flour. When she came home, she made the cake and invited her family and friends to celebrate.

They all sang. Sally cut the cake. She made sure that everyone had a slice.

Introducing

Call to Adventure

Call to Adventure

1. The **Call to Adventure** is when the hero decides to solve a conflict. The **conflict** can be emotional, physical, spiritual, external, etc. By answering the "call", the hero will always be challenged emotionally.

2. The call is an early part – beginning – of the hero's journey.

3. The **Call to Adventure** can happen at anytime: at the first page, or later, but closer to the beginning than the middle.

4. If the Protagonist does not accept the **Call to Adventure**, there is no story.

Notes to Teachers

The hero's journey and the call to adventure
   Suggested Reading:
   1. *The Writer's Journey* by Chris Vogler
   2. *Hero with a Thousand Faces* by Joseph Campbell

Call to Adventure – When it happens:
Something happens in the story that spurs the character to action: this is the Call to Adventure. How he answers that call is termed "the hero's journey."

For simplicity's sake, the stories in this workbook have their Call to Adventure near the beginning.

Call to Adventure – Refusal:
There are instances (often in film) where the character refuses the call and the story becomes the avoidance of the destiny (often with disastrous or tragic consequences). A story character can also refuse the first call—circumstances need to change before the hero accepts the Call to Adventure.

For example, the story of the Were-Tiger's sister. (Taken from *The Girl Sudan Painted Like A Gold Ring* by Theresa Fuller.) The Were-Tiger is a demonic spirit that beheads people. The Were-Tiger's sister detests her brother for his despicable deeds, but is unable to defy him until one day, Danjai, a Sea Dyak chief appears in her village. He is seeking revenge on the Were-Tiger for taking the head of his wife. With Danjai's help, the Were-Tiger's sister plots the demise of the Were-Tiger.

Call to Adventure – Confirmation:
Sometimes a hero needs confirmation that he is the chosen one.
In the Blibical story of Gideon, the hero – Gideon – is hiding from the Midianites when an angel speaks to him, calling him a mighty man of God and tells him that God has a mission for him: defeat

the Midianites. Gideon doubts that he is the right man for this mission. He asks for proof. Gideon uses a fleece as a sign. The first morning, Gideon wakes to find the fleece saturated with dew while the surrounding ground is dry. The second day, he awakes to find the fleece dry while the surrounding land is covered in dew. Believing now that he is called by God, Gideon accepts the Call and leads his army of men against the Midianites.

Call to Adventure – Detailed Setup:
In the world of film making, this Call to Adventure often comes after a detailed set-up, and it would also in some genres in the world of fiction. Certainly the Call would not happen "just before the middle." By this time the story is far advanced. But there are no hard absolutes in either film or books.

The hero's journey (his path following the call) was based on far earlier analysis of story needs, even before Joseph Campbell's book.

Call to Adventure – Disruption of the Ordinary World:
The Call to Adventure often disrupts the Ordinary World and establishes the stakes if it is rejected. After rejection, there is the acceptance that shows the hero's core values – what the hero is willing to suffer and sacrifice for it.

Call to Adventure – Switching of Goal:
There are many interesting angles to the hero's journey. Sometimes the hero switches his goal. The next page shows an example where the hero/protagonist switches his goal.

KING SOLOMON AND THE BABY

Two mothers once lived in the same house. During the night, one of the mothers rolled onto her baby and smothered it. The remaining baby was then claimed by both mothers.

The bickering women approached King Solomon. The first mother argued hard but so did the second mother that the remaining baby was hers.

The king called for a sword.

"Cut the baby in half," said King Solomon.

"Go ahead," said the first mother. "This way neither of us can have him."

"No, stop!" said the second mother. **"Let her have the baby."**

"Don't kill the baby," said the wise king. "Give the baby to the mother who begged to stop. She is the real mother."

And everyone in Israel was amazed at how the king had come to his decision.

QUESTIONS

1. Who is the protagonist?

2. When does the story take place?

3. Where is the story set?

4. What is the goal? Motivation?

5. Conflict?

6. What was the Call to Adventure?

7. What happened in the end (resolution)?

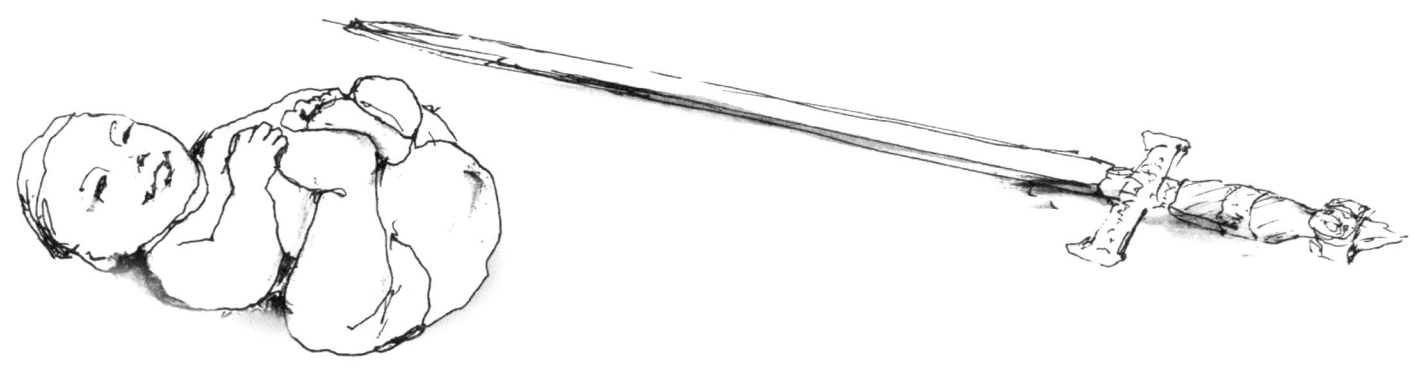

ANSWERS

1) The second mother. 2) The story takes place during the time of King Solomon. 3) The story is set in Israel. 4) The second mother wanted her baby. Why? Because she was the baby's mother. 5) The first mother wanted the baby, too. 6) At first they went to King Solomon to decide who the baby's mother was. 7) In the end, King Solomon called for a sword to divide the baby in half. The false mother agreed with the king's decision as she did not care if the baby died, but the baby's real mother (the second mother) begged the king to stop. She wanted the baby alive. Her decision proved that she was the real mother as only the real mother would care more about the baby being alive. She was willing to switch her goal to keep her child alive.

Introducing

Change of Plans

THE MIDDLE

Generally, the middle is often the most difficult part of any story to write. It shows how the protagonist tries to solve the problem.

And fails.

It shows the protagonist's reaction.

It includes the **CHANGE OF PLANS**.

The **CHANGE OF PLANS** is where the protagonist changes direction. Normally this is because he has failed or circumstances have changed and he must adapt. This change makes the story more interesting because he often goes in the opposite direction.

Writing Fact

The **Change of Plans** happens in the middle of the story. It divides the story.

Now *you* try.

THE THREE LITTLE PIGS

Once there were three little pigs, who decide to **leave home and seek their fortunes**, but their mother warned them that there was a Big Bad Wolf who would try to catch them.

The three little pigs met a man carrying straw.

"Can I please have some straw?" asked the first little pig. And the man let him have as much as he wanted.

And so, the first little pig built a house of straw.

"Goodbye brother! You have a fine house, and we hope you will be safe!" cried the second and third little pigs as they left their brother enjoying the comforts of his new house of straw.

Next, the two little pigs met a man carrying sticks.

"Can I please have some sticks?" asked the second little pig. And the man let him have as much as he wanted.

And so, the second little pig built a house of sticks.

"Goodbye brother! You have a fine house, and I hope you will be safe!" cried the third little pig as he left his brother enjoying the comforts of his house of sticks.

Next, the third little pig met a man carrying bricks.

"Can I please have some bricks?" asked the third little pig. And the man let him have as many as he wanted.

And so, the third little pig built a house of brick. And soon he was enjoying the comforts of his new house of brick.

But soon the Big Bad Wolf came along.

The Wolf came to the house of the first little pig.

"Little pig, little pig, let me come in!" cried the Wolf.

"Not by the hair of my chinny-chin-chin," said the first little pig.

"Then I'll huff and I'll puff, and I'll blow your house down!" cried the Big Bad Wolf. And he huffed and he puffed, and he blew the house of straw down.

As soon as the house of straw collapsed, the first little pig ran to the safety of the house of his second brother.

But the Big Bad Wolf came to the house of the second little pig.

"Little pigs, little pigs, let me come in!" cried the Wolf.

"Not by the hair of our chinny-chin-chins," said the first and the second little pigs.

"Then I'll huff and I'll puff, and I'll blow your house down!" cried the Big Bad Wolf. And he huffed and he puffed, and he blew the house of sticks down.

As soon as the house of sticks collapsed, the first and the second little pigs ran to the safety of the house of brick of their brother.

But the Big Bad Wolf also came to the house of the third little pig.

"Little pigs, little pigs, let me come in!" cried the Wolf.

"Not by the hair of our chinny-chin-chins," said the three little pigs.

"Then I'll huff and I'll puff, and I'll blow your house down!" cried the Big Bad Wolf. And he huffed and he puffed, but the house of brick still stood.

So the Big Bad Wolf tried again.

He huffed and he puffed, but the house of brick still stood!

The Big Bad Wolf tried for the third time.

He huffed and he puffed.

But the **HOUSE OF BRICK STILL STOOD**!

The Big Bad Wolf thought for a while. Then he climbed onto the roof of the house of bricks.

Inside the house, the three little pigs could hear the wolf on the roof.

They fetched a pot of hot water and lit the fire in the fireplace.

There was a sudden whoosh and then a horrible yowl as the wolf slid down the chimney straight into the boiling hot water. Splash!

With a howl, the wolf scuttled straight up the chimney.

The wolf ran away, never to return, and the three little pigs lived happily ever after, in the house of bricks.

QUESTIONS

1. Who is the protagonist?

2. When does the story take place?

3. Where is the story set?

4. What is the goal? Motivation?

5. Conflict?

6. How did they solve their problem (what steps did they take)?

7. What was the protagonist's reaction?

8. At which point did the Change of Plans occur?

9. What happened in the end (resolution)?

ANSWERS

1) The protagonists are the three little pigs. 2) The story takes place Once Upon a Time. 3) The story is set in a fantasy world.   4) The goal of the three little pigs is to seek adventure while staying alive. This second goal is implied. Motivation – no one wants to die.   5) The Big Bad Wolf wants to eat them. 6) First they built a house of straw, then a house of sticks and finally a house of bricks. Finally, they placed a pot of boiling water in the fireplace. 7) At first they taunted the wolf by saying "Not by the hair of my chinny-chin-chin."   8) The Change of Plans occurs when the wolf fails to demolish the brick house.   9) When the wolf is scalded by the hot water, he runs away.

NUKHUDU

A long time ago in ancient Persia, a shopkeeper sent word home to his wife for some broth.

The wife poured a bowlful of steaming broth then sighed. "If only I had a son who could carry this bowl for me to the bazaar."

No sooner had the woman spoken when a Pea hopped out of the soup.

"I am your son," said the Pea. "My name is Nukhudu. I will carry this bowl to my father."

At once the woman gave the bowl to the Pea and he hurried to the bazaar.

"I am your son, and here is your bowl of broth," said Nukhudu.

"I don't have a son," said the shopkeeper. "If you are really my son, then go to the Shah and demand that he return the copper coin that I lent him."

At once, **Nukhudu set off to the Shah's palace**.

As Nukhudu crossed the desert, a Jackal snarled, "Where are you going?"

"I am going to the Shah to demand that he return my father's copper coin," said Nukhudu.

"That I should like to see. Let me come with you," said the Jackal.

"You may. But we have a long journey. Jump into my mouth and I will carry you."

Nukhudu opened his mouth very wide, and the Jackal jumped in.

As Nukhudu crossed a hillside, a Leopard growled, "Where are you going?"

"I am going to the Shah to demand that he return my father's copper coin," said Nukhudu.

"That I should like to see. Let me come with you," said the Leopard.

"You may. But we have a long journey. Jump into my mouth and I will carry you."

Nukhudu opened his mouth very wide, and the Leopard jumped in.

As Nukhudu crossed a bridge, the Stream sang, "Where are you going?"

"I am going to the Shah to demand that he return my father's copper coin," said Nukhudu.

"That I should like to see. Let me come with you," said the Stream.

"You may. But we have a long journey. Jump into my mouth and I will carry you."

Nukhudu opened his mouth very wide, and the Stream jumped in.

At last Nukhudu arrived at the Shah's palace.

"Oh Shah! I have come to ask you to return the copper coin that my father lent you," said Nukhudu.

The Shah looked down mockingly at the little Pea. "Nonsense!" Then he turned to his Wazir. "Throw him to the fighting cocks!"

So Nukhudu was seized and thrown to the fighting cocks. But before the fighting cocks could pounce on the little Pea, Nukhudu cried out, "O Jackal! Come and save me!"

At once the Jackal leapt out and killed the fighting cocks.

When the Shah learnt what had happened to his prized fighting cocks he shook in anger.

"Throw him to the wild horses!" he said to his Wazir.

So Nukhudu was seized and thrown to the wild horses. But before the wild horses could trample the little Pea, Nukhudu cried out, "O Leopard! Come and save me!"

At once the Leopard leapt out and killed the wild horses.

The Shah seethed with rage when he discovered what Nukhudu had done.

"Fill a room with straw. Set fire to it then throw him into that room."

So Nukhudu was seized and thrown into the burning room. But before the fire could consume the little Pea, Nukhudu cried out, "O Stream! Come and save me!"

At once the Stream leapt out and drowned the fire.

The Shah's anger turned to despair when he heard what Nukudu had done.

"What shall we do?" he asked his Wazir.

"The only thing. Let him into the Treasury to find his father's copper coin."

Nukhudu was let into the Treasury. There he ran about gulping down as much gold and jewels as he could. Finally, when he could hold no more, he picked up a little copper coin, and twirling it over the back of his fingers, he ran out. "I have my father's coin!"

No one stopped him as he ran back across the bridge.

No one stopped him as he ran back across the hillside.

No one stopped him as he ran back across the desert.

When Nukhudu reached home, he called out, "Mother! Hang me upside down and beat me!"

His astonished mother did as he asked, and as she beat Nukhudu with a stick, all the gold and precious jewels began to pour from Nukhudu's mouth.

So the delighted shopkeeper and wife became very rich and they lived happily together with their new son, Nukhudu, whom they loved very much.

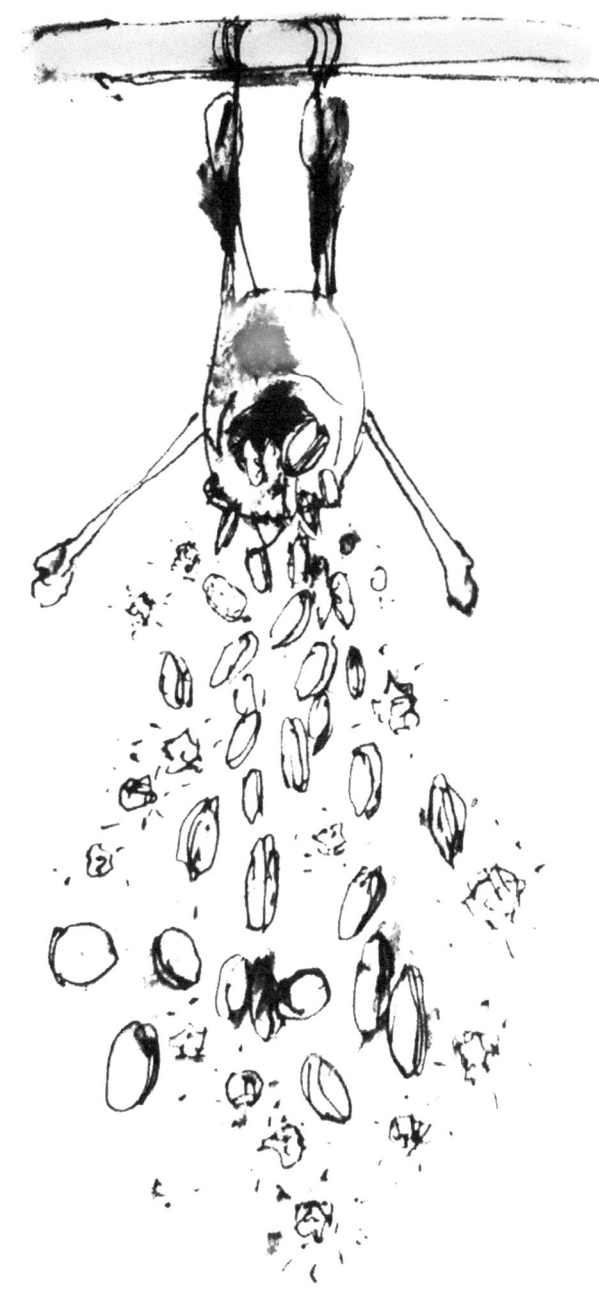

Questions

1. Who is the protagonist?

2. When does the story take place?

3. Where is the story set?

4. What is the goal? Motivation?

5. Conflict?

6. How did they solve their problem (what steps did they take)?

7. What was the protagonist's reaction?

8. At which point did the Change of Plans occur?

9. What happened in the end (resolution)?

Answers

1) Nukhudu is the protagonist. 2) The story takes place a long time ago. 3) The story is set in ancient Persia which is today's Iran and Iraq. 4) Nukhudu's goal is to collect the copper coin. His motivation is to prove to his father that he is a son worth having, even though he is a Pea. 5) The conflict is when the Shah refuses to return the copper coin and tries to get rid of Nukhudu. 6) Nukhudu accepts the help of everyone who wishes to assist. 7) Nukhudu accepts calmly what he has to do. 8) Before Nukhudu reached the Shah's palace he was in control. He could open his mouth to swallow the Jackal, the Leopard and the Stream, but after Nukhudu arrives at the Palace, things appear out of his control (Change of Plans). He has to ask his friends to save him. 9) In the end, Nukhudu is allowed into the Treasury to collect the coin. His father accepts him.

NOTES TO TEACHERS

Stories may relate to or overlap with one in which the protagonist learns a lesson rather than meets a goal. The story on the following page is one such example.

Some may call it a tragedy.

The Gingerbread Man

Once an old lady made a Gingerbread Man. As she opened the oven, out popped the Gingerbread Man.

"Catch me if you can! I can run so fast because I'm the Gingerbread Man!" laughed the Gingerbread Man as he ran away.

As the Gingerbread Man runs, he comes across an old man, an old woman and a little boy.

The old man tries to catch him but fails.

The old lady tries to catch him but fails.

The little boy tries to catch him but fails.

Each time someone tries to catch him, the Gingerbread Man sings out, "Hahahahahahaha! Catch me if you can! I can run so fast because I'm the Gingerbread Man!"

Then the Gingerbread Man comes across a fox.

"Hahahahahahaha! Catch me if you can! I can run so fast because I'm the Gingerbread Man!"

Only the fox doesn't run after the Gingerbread Man.

"I can't quite hear you, Gingerbread Man. Won't you come a little closer," says the fox in a feeble voice.

The Gingerbread Man stops running for the first time.

"I have outrun an old man, an old lady and a little boy, and I can outrun you, too-o-o!" sings the Gingerbread Man.

"I can't quite hear you, Gingerbread Man. Won't you come a little closer," says the fox, putting one paw behind his ear.

The Gingerbread Man comes closer for the first time. "Hahahahahahaha! Catch me if you can! I can run so fast because I'm the Gingerbread Man!"

The fox snaps up the Gingerbread Man and that is the end of him!

QUESTIONS

1. Who is the protagonist/character?

2. When does the story take place?

3. Where is the story set?

4. What is the goal? Motivation?

5. Conflict?

6. How did they solve their problem (what steps did they take)?

7. What was the protagonist's reaction?

8. At which point did the Change of Plans occur? (Hint: Up until this point everyone has been trying to catch the Gingerbread Man.)

9. What happened in the end (resolution)?

ANSWERS

1) The protagonist is the Gingerbread Man. 2) The story takes place Once upon a Time. 3) The story is set in another fantasy world. 4) To outrun everyone. It is assumed that it is to live, but here the Gingerbread Man is so boastful that it seems it is more interested in outrunning others than staying alive. 5) The Gingerbread Man is delicious and so everyone wants to eat it. 6) He ran faster than the others. 7) At first the reaction of the Gingerbread Man is to run. 8) The Change of Plans happens when the Gingerbread Man meets the fox. The fox doesn't try to chase him, and so doesn't appear to want to eat him. 9) In the end, the Gingerbread Man goes towards the fox and is eaten.

Notes to Teachers

Tragedy is an event and it is also the term used to identify a certain style of drama and literature. One of the most evocative literary concepts is — "tragedy". What happened to the gingerbread man is—for him—a tragedy of events, but it is not a fictional (work of) "tragedy".

A tragedy can be an event; (such as the destruction caused by World War One).

A tragedy can be a literary form – tragic drama – Shakespeare's play *Hamlet* is a classic example. Homer's Illiad is a tragedy (literature/poetry).

The Gingerbread Man is a parable or a fable depending on whether one sees the gingerbread man as animalistic or "human".

Tragedy can make for memorable fiction.

A story can make an emotional connection between the characters and their readers. Tragic events can make a work memorable, but only if the reader has a connection with the character/s.

Aristotle states in his *Poetics* circa 335 BC that the purpose of tragedy is to arouse the emotions of pity and fear, and thereby effect the catharsis of these emotions. Arouse these sensations and then purge them, so we feel cleansed and uplifted and with a heightened sense of the ways of gods and men.

Tragedy in literature often imparts knowledge.

The following story, *The Crane Wife*, is a favourite Japanese tragedy. The truth is that tragedies may stay with us, as they can often strike at the heart of humanity. They often terrify.

Note:

A fable is generally a fictitious story that conveys a moral. The characters are often animals. An example is Belling the Cat.

A parable is a simple story that has a spiritual or moral lesson. An example is *The Boy Who Cried Wolf*.

THE CRANE WIFE

A long time ago in Japan, a man once found an injured crane on his doorstep.

Believing the bird had been shot by hunters, the man takes the poor creature into his home, where he nurses and cares for the bird until it is well enough to leave. The next day he releases the crane.

That night, the man finds a beautiful girl on his doorstep who tells him that she would like to become his wife. When the man tells her that he cannot afford to support a wife, the girl says that she can weave splendid clothing that he will be able to sell for a great price. The only condition is that the man is never to look inside the room while she is weaving.

As the man has fallen in love with the girl, **he readily promises**.

The new wife goes into the room and each morning emerges with a wonderful garment which the man takes to market and sells for a huge amount of money. His wife does this every single night and each morning presents her husband with a gorgeous piece of clothing. But each day she is exhausted and thinner.

Finally, curiosity gets the better of the husband. Even though his wife has warned him never to peek into the room, **he decides to spy on his wife**.

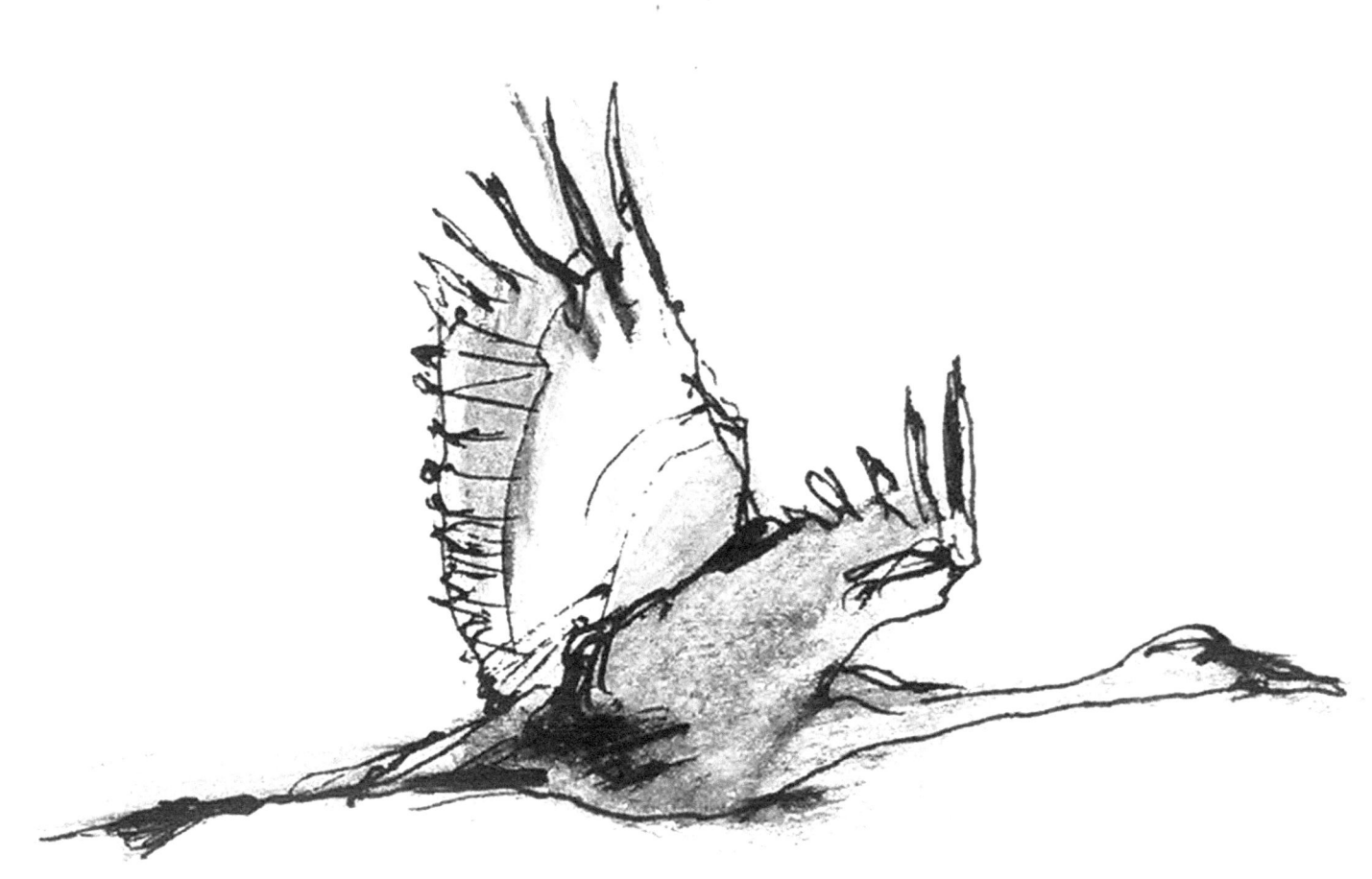

That night, when she goes into the room, he peers through a hole in the wall. To his astonishment, instead of his wife at the loom, he sees a large white crane. The bird is plucking feathers from its body and weaving them into material as it weeps. Shocked, the man recognizes the injured bird he took care of.

The crane looks up and sees the man. As the husband has broken the promise he made to his wife, and as he now knows the crane's identity, it gives him one forlorn look before flying away.

The crane wife never returns.

QUESTIONS

1. Who is the protagonist/character?

2. When does the story take place?

3. Where is the story set?

4. What is the goal? Motivation?

5. Conflict?

6. How did they solve their problem (what steps did they take)?

7. What was the protagonist's reaction?

8. At which point did the Change of Plans occur?

9. What happened in the end (resolution)?

ANSWERS

1) The protagonist is the man in the story. 2) The story takes place Once upon a Time. 3) The story is set in mythical Japan. 4) The man's goal is to earn a living. If he has sufficient money, he can keep his wife. 5) He does not earn enough to be able to support his wife. 6) His wife will weave clothes that the man can sell for a great price. 7) At first the man obeyed his wife's warning. 8) The Change of Plans occurs when the man becomes curious. Up until now he has obeyed his wife's instructions never to look inside the room. 9) In the end, the man looks inside the room and sees the crane he has rescued. The crane discovers his betrayal and flies away, never to return.

Consolidation *of the beginning & middle*

Narrative = story

3 main parts.
- beginning
- middle
- end

Beginning:
- hero/protagonist/character
- goal
- motivation
- conflict
- setting
- when
- call to adventure

Middle:
- how
- change of plans

End:
- resolution

Introducing

The Climax

THE RESOLUTION

The beginning of the End:

- **THE CLIMAX** is the scene where the main tensions of the story are brought to their most intense point i.e. the big showdown.

- After **THE CLIMAX** the protagonist is (normally) left as a better person, or is changed by his adventure.

- The Resolution is where the story is complete.

- Stories come in many forms and endings can vary between the different story genres (fantasy, romance, horror, for example). Some have HEA (happily ever after) endings, others have tragic endings. Often the readers of certain genres have expectations as to the acceptable and/or anticipated ending.

Writing Fact

To Save the day the **protagonist** must dig deep – mentally, physically, emotionally, spiritually – often at his own expense. That is why he is called a **"hero"**.

Introducing

The Antagonist

The Antagonist

The Antagonist can be the enemy (villain); he can also be the antithesis of the hero, or he can be a "foil".

The antagonist is the person or thing that challenges the hero and stands between the hero and his goal. Rarely in fictional stories is **The Antagonist** a thing (an animal or a natural force) that the hero must overcome.

Often **The Antagonist** is an enemy of the hero (or he soon becomes the enemy due to the conflict between them); he is the antithesis of all the hero stands for. **The Antagonist** must be equal to, or sometimes more powerful than the protagonist.

Why?

So that when the hero prevails against his nemesis it is a triumph!

Now *you* try.

Find the **antagonist** and the **climax**.

THE OLD MAN OF THE SEA

On Sinbad's fifth voyage, he ended up shipwrecked on an island. As Sinbad walked about the island, he found a wonderful orchard full of delicious fruit. He ate his fill and continued his exploration.

Under the branches of a tree, Sinbad found **an old man** with crippled legs.

Thinking he is another shipwrecked victim, Sinbad lifts the man onto his shoulders so he can gather fruit.

But when Sinbad asked the old man to come down the man refuses.

Although Sinbad tries repeatedly, he cannot get the old man to release his grip on him. Sinbad is forced to sleep with the old man hanging on.

The old man forces Sinbad to carry him about. Slowly, Sinbad grows weaker and weaker.

Finally, Sinbad realises that the old man would rather let Sinbad die than release him.

Sinbad comes up with a plan.

Sinbad found a gourd which he hollowed out. Next he gathered grapes. He squeezed the juice of the grapes into the gourd and allowed it to ferment.

When the juice turned into wine, Sinbad was ready.

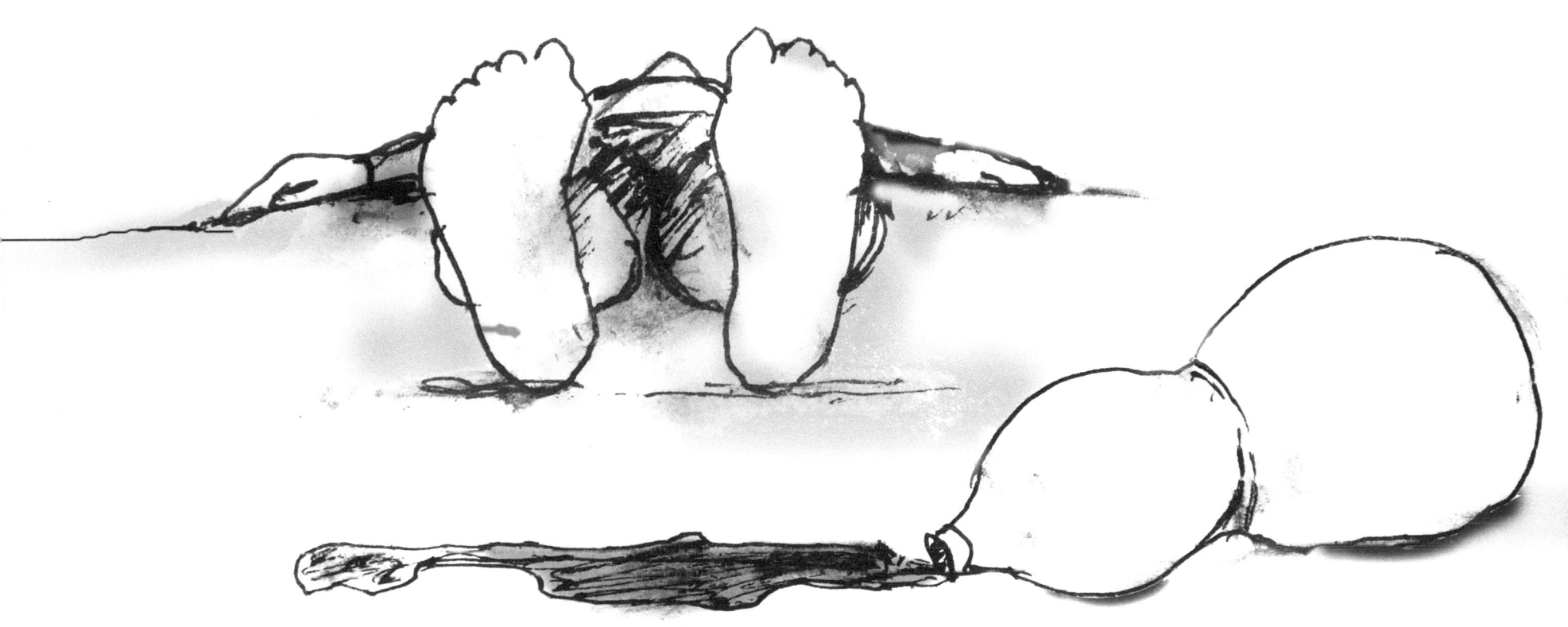

He started to drink the wine and made a great show of enjoying himself.

Seeing Sinbad so joyous, the old man asked for some of the wine. At first Sinbad refused to hand the gourd over, but then he appeared to relent.

He gave the old man the gourd.

At once the greedy old man gulped all the wine down. But that was Sinbad's plan.

Soon the wine took effect and the old man became drunk. He released his grip on Sinbad and Sinbad was able to escape.

Sinbad ran for the beach where he hailed a passing ship and returned home to Baghdad.

QUESTIONS

1. Who is the protagonist?

2. When does the story take place?

3. Where is the story set?

4. What is the goal? Motivation?

5. What is the conflict? And who is the Antagonist?

6. How did Sinbad try to solve the problem at first?

7. What was the protagonist's reaction?

8. At which point did the Change of Plans occur?

9. What happens at the climax?

10. What happened in the end (resolution)?

ANSWERS

1) Sinbad is the protagonist. 2) The story takes place on Sinbad's 5th voyage. 3) On an unknown island. 4) Sinbad's goal is to escape the Old Man of the Sea. He is motivated to save his own life. 5) The Old Man of the Sea is the antagonist. He needs Sinbad's legs to move around and refuses to release him. 6) At first Sinbad used reasoning and then brute force to free himself but when neither worked, he used his guile – he tricked the old man into becoming drunk. 7) Sinbad was shocked at being tricked. 8) The Change of Plans occurs when the old man refuses to release Sinbad. Sinbad then stops helping and instead comes up with a plan to get rid of the old man. 9) Sinbad has to trick the old man into wanting to drink the wine. If he fails he will die. 10) In the end, Sinbad gets the Old Man of the Sea drunk. When the Old Man falls down unconscious, Sinbad is free. He runs to the beach, hails a passing ship and returns home to Baghdad.

HANSEL AND GRETEL

Once upon a time, there lived in Germany a poor woodcutter, his wife and their two children, Hansel and Gretel. When a famine spreads over the land, the woodcutter's wife tells her husband that he must take the children deep into the woods to lose them as they eat too much. At first the woodcutter refuses to do so, but then the day comes when they are down to their last crust of bread.

Hansel overhears his **parents** plotting. Before sunrise the next day, Hansel gathers as many white pebbles as he can.

Their parents pretend to take the children for a walk, but instead abandon them.

When Gretel cries, Hansel tells her not to worry. They just need to wait. When the moon rises it shines on the white pebbles. Now the children can follow the trail.

When the children return, they find that their parents have food so it is a joyous reunion. But when the food runs out once more, the woodcutter's wife decides that they must abandon the children again. This time she locks the door so that Hansel cannot go out to gather pebbles.

As the children set out for the woods a second time, Hansel and Gretel are each given a crust of bread. While Gretel eats hers, Hansel saves his, breaking off pieces to make a trail. The children are left deeper in the woods, but this time Gretel does not cry. She knows that all they must do is wait for the moon to rise.

But when the moon rises, there is no trail of breadcrumbs.

The birds have eaten the bread.

The two children wander about lost in the woods until they come to a strange house made of gingerbread, cookies, cakes and candy and windows of clear sugar.

The children break off pieces and are eating when the owner of the house comes out.

The owner is a **witch**.

She locks Hansel in a cage and forces Gretel to cook and clean.

Each morning, the witch asks Hansel to stick his finger out so she can see how fat he has grown. But her vision is poor and when Hansel sticks a bone out, she believes he is too thin to eat.

After several weeks, the witch loses patience. She declares that she will eat Hansel the next day be he lean or fat.

By now the witch is preparing to eat both Hansel and Gretel.

The witch tells Gretel to lean over the open oven to see if the fire is hot enough only Gretel pretends not to understand. Angry that Gretel does not know what to do, the witch leans over to demonstrate.

At once, Gretel shoves the witch into the hot oven and slams the door shut. Gretel frees Hansel.

The two children explore the witch's house before they leave. They find inside the house many treasures and they fill their pockets.

A white swan gives them a ride across the lake and in a short time the children are back at the cottage. Their mother is dead.

Their father is delighted to have his children back safe again. And they all live happily ever after.

QUESTIONS

1. Who are the protagonists?

2. When does the story take place?

3. Where is the story set?

4. What is the goal? Motivation?

5. Conflict? Initial antagonists?

6. How did they solve their problem (what steps did they take)?

7. What was the protagonists' reaction?

8. At which point did the Change of Plans occur?

9. What happens at the climax?

10. What happened in the end (resolution)?

ANSWERS

1) Hansel and Gretel are the protagonists. 2) The story takes place Once Upon a Time. 3) The story is set in mythical Germany. 4) The goal of the children is to return home. 5) The parents cannot afford to feed them and so abandon them. 6) At first all the children need to do is find the way back home but then they are caught by the witch. 7) The children are sad to be abandoned. 8) At first the children work at simply trying to get home. The Change of Plans occurs when they meet the witch who traps them. Each time the children are in trouble it has always been Hansel who has saved them but now Hansel is locked in a cage. It is Gretel who has to save them both. And now the witch wants to eat Hansel. 9) After several weeks, the witch loses patience as Hansel does not appear to be getting fatter. The climax occurs when she tells Gretel to check if the oven is hot enough, hoping to trick the girl. It is a terrifying moment but instead, it is the witch who is tricked. Gretel pretends not to understand the witch's instructions. Frustrated, the witch leans over the hot oven, Gretel pushes the witch into the oven and slams the door shut. The witch is dead. 10) In the end, Gretel frees Hansel. The two children fill their pockets with the treasure that the witch has stolen from her victims and return in triumph to their father.

Notes to Teachers

Does the hero always win?

No. Actually in some genres he loses and this causes him internal and external conflicts: his redemption is part of the story.

While the hero may fail, each narrative must present a reason for that failure in order to provide the reader with a satisfying ending.

In the original version of *The Little Mermaid*, the protagonist does not win the love of the prince. Instead the prince goes on to marry someone else.

How many of us remember the agony of waiting for a special occasion as a child and thus we empathise by suffering with her as she waits for the chance to see the upper world. We admire her courage as she strives to save the prince and later as she journeys to the Sea Witch's house to obtain the potion that she needs to give her legs. When she falls in love with the prince, we fall along side her. How many of us can relate to the pain of unrequited love?

We hope repeatedly as she does her best, hampered by the lack of her most beautiful asset – her voice – to make the prince fall in love with her. How many of us understand what it is like to go through life handicapped in some form or other?

We shake our heads in disbelief when we discover that the prince has instead decided to marry someone else. We cry out in our hearts that this is a mistake. That surely he can see the love shining in the Little Mermaid's eyes. We all understand disappointment too well.

We, too, are numb at the discovery of what the Little Mermaid must do in order to live. Can she undertake that monstrous deed? The alternative is too dreadful to contemplate.

We weep as the Little Mermaid throws herself into the sea.

Then rejoice at her second chance.

The story on the following pages is a short adaptation. Read the full story to understand how Andersen achieves his aim for us to fall in love with the Little Mermaid.

Written in 1837, of all his stories, this is the one that resonated the most with his readers. It led to the construction of the iconic Little Mermaid Statue in Copenhagen Harbour in 1913.

Now *you* try.

THE ORIGINAL LITTLE MERMAID

The Underwater Kingdom lies in hidden seas, below waters clear as crystal. There in a great castle with amber windows, where fish swim in and out like swallows, dwells the Merking and his six daughters. While the older five are exceedingly beautiful it is the youngest – the Little Mermaid – who is the most enchanting.

On the day each daughter turns fifteen, the young princess is taken to the surface to view the upper world. The Little Mermaid, being the youngest, must wait the longest while her older sisters take their turns. And as each returns to reveal their discoveries, to talk of lying on a sandbank in moonlight, or of icebergs glittering like pearls or how the whole sky shone like gold, the Little Mermaid sighs longingly and grows more and more impatient.

Finally, five years pass, and her time comes.

With a wreath of white lilies in her hair, the Little Mermaid rises to the surface. She finds herself drawn to a birthday celebration for a young prince taking place on board a royal ship. Soon she falls in love with the handsome prince with coal black eyes. The celebrations are halted when a storm hits.

As the ship sinks, the Little Mermaid swims among the planks and beams, knowing that she could be crushed but desperate to find the prince. Exhausted, his eyes closed, he is fast disappearing beneath the waves. The Little Mermaid holds his head high above the tempestuous sea and delivers him to shore. As she waits for him to revive, she kisses his high forehead and smooths back his wet hair. How she wishes that he would wake, but the prince remains unconscious. Soon the sweet sounds of bells drifts over the tops of the orange groves. As a young woman descends from the nearby temple the Little Mermaid hides among high rocks out at sea. While she is glad to see the young woman approach, the Little Mermaid is forlorn that the prince never opens his eyes to see her. Or know that it was she who saved him. Only when he revives can she finally tear herself away, the sight of the prince smiling at the young woman burning in her memory.

Having lost her heart to the human prince, the Little Mermaid despairs of ever seeing him again. She wonders if humans who do not drown would live forever. Her grandmother who wears twelve oysters on her tail explains that mermaids live for three hundred years, while humans' lives are much shorter. However, humans have an immortal soul that lives on in heaven, whereas mermaids turn into sea foam when they die.

Longing to see the prince again and dreaming of an eternal soul, the Little Mermaid visits the sea witch to obtain a potion that will give her legs. She finds the sea witch in a house made from the bones of human beings who have drowned. The sea witch warns the Little Mermaid that once she becomes human she can never return to the ocean. She may have two legs but each time she walks she will feel as if she is treading on sharp knives. But that is not all. Her life is forfeit until she can win the love of the young prince and marry him. For should he marry someone else, the Little Mermaid will dissolve into sea foam.

Despite the warning, the Little Mermaid agrees. She sticks out her little pink tongue as payment which the sea witch promptly cuts off.

Sad to leave her family and home forever, the Little Mermaid swims to the surface and drinks the potion. Pain pierces through her body like a two-edged sword.

But the potion does what the witch promised. When the Little Mermaid recovers, she has two legs. She is found by the prince, but as she opens her mouth, realises to her grief that she is mute.

In the palace, the Little Mermaid is dressed in costly robes of gold and silk. She must now endeavour to do all in her power to win the heart of the prince. The Little Mermaid hears others singing in the throne room to the king and queen. One sings better than the rest. When the prince applauds the singer, the Little Mermaid grieves, knowing that her own voice was far better, and that she had given it away to be with him. When others dance, she too dances, waving her white arms and gliding over the floor despite daggers stabbing the soles of her feet. She is the best dancer of them all and the prince praises her and calls her his foundling.

The prince and the Little Mermaid grow close. They ride horses and climb mountains and with each step the Little Mermaid suffers because she is by his side. As the days pass the prince loves her more and more, but only as a friend. Despite the love that shines from her eyes, he decides to marry the girl from the temple, believing her to be his true rescuer from drowning.

As perfumed oil burns in silver lamps on every alter, the prince and his new bride celebrate their marriage. The Little Mermaid realises that she has failed. She is numb at the thought of turning into sea foam at daybreak. But before morning her five sisters arrive.

With pale faces, they present the Little Mermaid with a knife.

Shocked, the Little Mermaid discovers that they have sacrificed their long beautiful hair in exchange for the knife. But she is even more stunned to learn what it is that they are urging her to do. For the Little Mermaid must use the knife to kill the prince.

Only when his warm blood drips onto her legs will she become a mermaid again and she can then live out the rest of her life with her family.

The Little Mermaid does not want to die.

She goes to the bedroom of the prince, but when she pulls aside the crimson curtain and sees the prince's sleeping face, she realises that she loves him still.

The Little Mermaid throws away the knife.

Then she plunges into the ocean.

But instead of vanishing, or dying, the Little Mermaid feels the heat of the sun on her body and finds herself becoming lighter. Then she notices transparent beings all around her.

The Little Mermaid has turned into a luminous daughter of the air. Although she did not win the prince's love, because of the pain she endured and because of her longing for an immortal soul, she has been given a second chance.

Thus, the Little Mermaid can one day rise to unknown and glorious regions. And live forever in that ethereal world among the stars.

QUESTIONS

1. Who is the protagonist?

2. When does the story take place?

3. Where is the story set?

4. What is the goal? Motivation?

5. Conflict? Antagonist?

6. How did she solve their problem (what steps did she take)?

7. What was the protagonist's reaction?

8. At which point did the Change of Plans occur?

9. What happens at the climax?

10. What happened in the end (resolution)?

ANSWERS

1) The Little Mermaid is the protagonist. 2) The story takes place Once Upon a Time. 3) The story is set in a fantasy world. 4) The goal of the Little Mermaid is to make the prince fall in love with her because she loves him. 5) Conflict: She has no legs. The Antagonist is the second woman whom the prince sees on waking up. 6) She visits the sea witch to ask for legs. 7) The Little Mermaid is sad to leave her family and home. 8) The Change of Plans occurs when she obtains her legs and finally meets the prince. 9) At the climax, the prince marries the princess. The Little Mermaid is then presented with a dreadful option – she can save her life if she kills the prince. But the Little Mermaid truly loves the prince and so she discards this option. 10) In the end, the Little Mermaid is given another chance. She becomes a luminous daughter of the air.

Puteri Gunung Ledang

Sultan Mansur Shah had heard of the beauty of the celestial princess of Gunung Ledang. He sent his best warriors, led by the legendary Hang Tuah, to ask for the princess's hand in marriage.

As the men climbed the mountain a strong wind struck up, but the men persisted. They passed the singing bamboo, and when they had reached almost to the clouds, they found themselves in a fairy garden. Here they saw birds listening to the heavenly sounds, unafraid of any predators, so entranced were they by the unearthly music. Four women sat in this ethereal grove.

The men told the women of the Rajah of Malacca's desire to wed the princess. Late that night the men were given the first of seven conditions.

The first was to build a bridge of gold from Gunung Ledang to Malacca. After a long while, the men returned to tell the Sultan that the task was completed.

The second task was to build a bridge of silver from Malacca to Gunung Ledang.

Against great odds, this, too, was accomplished.

The third condition was to present seven trays of mosquito hearts to the princess. The fourth was to present seven trays of the hearts of mites.

The fifth task was to obtain a vat of water from dried areca leaves.

The sixth was to offer the princess a cup of the Sultan's blood.

At a tremendous cost to the Sultan's kingdom, all these tasks were accomplished.

Lastly, the seventh was for a cup of blood from the Sultan's infant son.

His only child.

When the foolish Sultan heard this request, he finally realised that he would never marry the princess.

"My kingdom is in ruins," said the Sultan. "Tell me, was she beautiful?"

"We never saw her face," said Hang Tuah.

QUESTIONS

1. Who is the protagonist?

2. When does the story take place?

3. Where is the story set?

4. What is the goal? Motivation?

5. Conflict? Antagonist(s)? (Hint: there can be more than one antagonist).

6. How did they solve their problem (what steps did they take)?

7. What was the protagonist's reaction?

8. At which point did the Change of Plans occur?

9. What happens at the climax?

10. What happened in the end (resolution)?

ANSWERS

1) Sultan Mansur Shah is the protagonist. 2) The story takes place Once Upon a Time. 3) The story is set in Gunung Ledang. 4) The Sultan's goal is to marry the princess, Puteri, of Gunung Ledang. He is motivated by her beauty and his pride. 5) The princess, Puteri Gunung Ledang, does not wish to marry the Sultan. The antagonists are the princess and the four women. 6) The Sultan met all of the princess's conditions except the very last one. He did not marry the princess in the end. 7) The Sultan was foolish enough to believe that he would succeed in the end. 8) The Change of Plans occurs when the Sultan learned of the final task. He is brought to his senses and accepts the futility of his request. 9) At the climax, the Sultan learned that he has failed. There is nothing more that can be done. 10) In the end, the disappointed Sultan hopes to gain some comfort from the princess's beauty but even in this he is thwarted.

The Weeping Lady

Meng Jiang Nu was not born in the usual way. Instead, when Old Meng and his neighbour, Old Jiang, cut open a gourd that had been growing on a wall between their two properties, the two men were surprised to find a baby girl staring back at them, her face as round as the pale moon.

As the two men and their wives had no children of their own, they decided to raise the child together. They named the baby Meng Jiang, after the two men, and Nu because that was the word for girl.

Meng Jiang Nu grew up beautiful and gracious. Everyone who met her loved her.

One day, when Meng Jiang Nu was bathing in the pond in the garden, she heard a noise. She was shocked to find a young man blushing as he stared at her.

His name was Wan Xi Liang.

"Forgive me," he said to the startled girl. "I was hiding from the emperor's soldiers."

At once Meng Jiang Nu understood what was happening.

In those days, the Chinese emperor Qin Shi Huang (221 BC-206 BC) had ordered a great wall to be built to stop the marauders from pillaging the land. Men from every village had been conscripted to construct this wall. Many did not return.

Meng Jiang Nu and her two families decided to hide Wan Xi Liang. Soon the teenage pair fell in love.

Despite knowing the danger of marrying Wan Xi Liang, Meng Jiang Nu insisted that she would marry no one else. But their happiness was cut short when three days after the wedding, soldiers burst in to remove the young husband.

For one year, the heart-broken Meng Jiang Nu waited in vain for her husband to return.

Then one cold night, she had a dreadful premonition. She dreamt she saw her husband crying out, "Cold, cold, cold."

Taking the warm clothes she had sewn for him, Meng Jiang Nu at once set off for the Great Wall.

She travelled for almost a year until she reached the wall. When she arrived, she begged for news of her husband. Everyone reacted to the name Wan Xi Liang with shock and horror.

Finally, one old man told her the truth.

Her husband had been specially selected for the Great Wall because of his name. It was rumoured that to prevent the wall from collapsing, a man needed to be buried for every mile. And Wan Xi Liang's name meant 'Ten thousand.'

Meng Jiang Nu wept as she realised that her husband was dead and that she would never see him again. Crying heartrendingly for three whole days and nights, she hit the wall repeatedly with her fists, at times pressing herself against the structure, as if trying to touch her beloved's face.

Finally, at dawn on the fourth day, there was the sound of a tremendous cracking. The earth shook and the wall vibrated for several minutes. Workers looked up in horror to see a section of the wall collapsing to reveal mounds of bones.

The emperor Qin Shi Huang was visiting the wall that day. Angered to discover what had happened, he ordered that the culprit be brought to him for immediate punishment, but on seeing Meng Jiang Nu, he was entranced by her beauty, and instead decided to marry her.

The teenage widow knew she could never marry the murderer of her husband, but she had a plan. She demanded three things of the emperor before she would agree to marry.

"First, my husband's bones must be found," said the young widow.

The emperor was so besotted with her rare beauty that he immediately agreed. Great chunks of the wall were torn down until finally the bones of Wan Xi Liang were found.

But still, the determined Meng Jiang Nu refused to marry the emperor.

"Next a grand funeral must be held in my husband's honour. And you and your entire court is to mourn."

Although the emperor hated the thought of mourning for a commoner, he agreed. A grand funeral was held in Wan Xi Liang's honour.

But when the emperor sent for the young bride, once more she refused to share his bed.

"Prepare a fine dragon robe, which you must don. Then we shall go on a trip to the sea," she said.

Believing that Meng Jiang Nu was finally going to be his, the emperor agreed. But when the robe was presented to him, to his shock he found that it was a mourning robe.

Enraged, the emperor confronted Meng Jiang Nu, but was instead scolded by her.

Before he could seize her, she cast herself into the sea. At once the emperor ordered his men to dredge the ocean but Meng Jiang Nu's actions had raised so much sympathy, not just among the people but also among the immortals. The Dragon King of the Sea and his daughter, the Dragon Princess, ordered their army of shrimps and crabs to raise a storm.

The emperor's men were defeated.

The foolish emperor never saw Meng Jiang Nu again.

QUESTIONS

1. Who is the protagonist?

2. When does the story take place?

3. Where is the story set?

4. What is the goal? Motivation?

5. Conflict? Antagonist?

6. How did they solve their problem (what steps did they take)?

7. What was the protagonist's reaction?

8. At which point did the Change of Plans occur?

9. What happens at the climax?

10. What happened in the end (resolution)? Is the ending satisfying?

ANSWERS

1) Meng Jiang Nu is the protagonist. 2) The story takes place between 221 BC–206 BC. 3) The story is set in mythical China. 4) In the beginning, Meng Jiang Nu's goal is to save her husband. She is motivated by love. 5) The problem is that Wan Xi Liang has been conscripted to build the wall. The antagonist is the Emperor Qin Shi Huang. 6) She gathered up the clothes she had made and journeyed to the wall. When she reached the wall, she tried to find her husband. But when she discovered that her husband was dead, her goal changed to one of vengeance. 7) Shock. She knew she could not marry the emperor. 8) The Change of Plans occurred when Meng Jiang Nu discovered her husband was dead. 9) At the climax, she has to prevent the emperor from marrying her while she seeks vengeance. 10) In the end, although Meng Jiang Nu does not get her husband back alive, she is able to obtain revenge on the foolish emperor. The story is a tragedy and so the ending is as satisfying as tragedies go.

Consolidation *of the narrative*

Narrative = story
3 main parts.
- beginning
- middle
- end

Beginning:
- hero/protagonist/character
- goal
- motivation
- conflict
- setting
- when
- call to adventure

Middle:
- how
- change of plans

End:
- the climax
- resolution

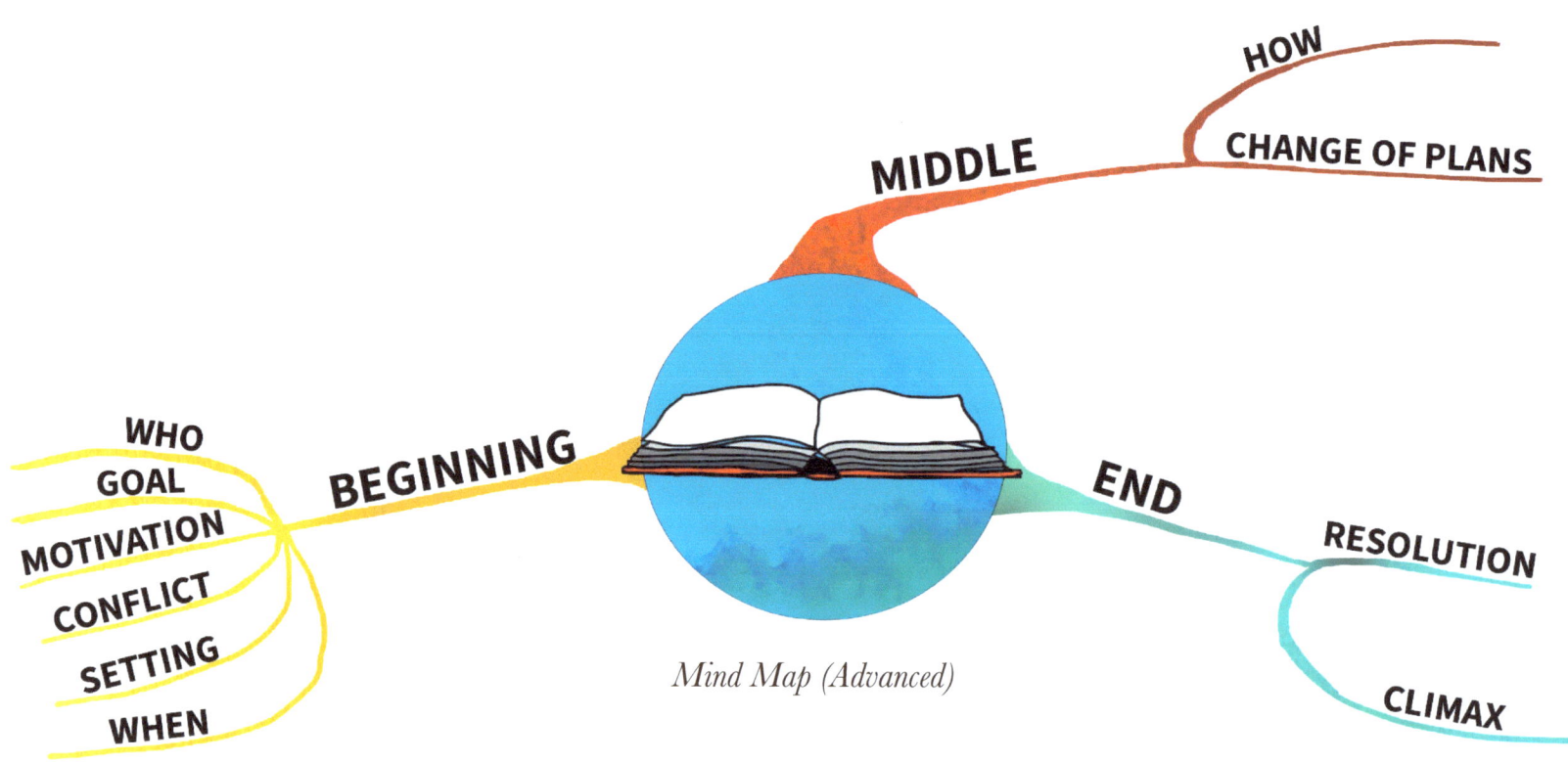

Mind Map (Advanced)

Now it's *your* turn.

About the Author

Theresa Fuller has always loved stories and story-telling, but it was not until the birth of her first son that she became a full-time writer. Her aim was to write stories about her culture: Southeast Asia.

Theresa has a degree in computing and was Head of Computing at various private schools in Sydney. She has also been a Higher School Certificate (HSC) Examiner and HSC Assessor. Her teaching degrees have seen her work in primary and secondary schools and at Kalgoorlie College in Western Australia.

Her first published novel in 2018 was *The Ghost Engine*, a steampunk fantasy about the fictitious granddaugher of Ada Lovelace, the world's first programmer. Theresa has published two books on Southeast Asian mythology: *The Girl Who Became A Goddess* (A collection of folktales from Singapore, Malaysia and China) in 2019 and *The Girl Sudan Painted Like A Gold Ring* in 2022. During the 2021 lockdown in Sydney, she, like many other parents, was forced to homeschool her children. When she discovered there was a scarcity of resources about narrative, the idea of writing her own resource book began to take hold. She remembered how hard it was to learn about narrative as a new writer, and wished that there had been a book that visually showed how narrative could be broken up. This workbook is the result.

Theresa will continue to write stories and her current mission is to help save the language of her ancestors – Baba Malay.

www.theresafuller.com

Acknowledgements

This book would not have been possible without the financial support of my husband, Paul. I am especially grateful to the three editors who have been supportive of my goal in creating a text for children and for beginner writers, and who worked tirelessly to provide me with the very best advice. Heartfelt thanks to Karen Albright Lin, Dayna Hart and to Gillian.

Thanks to Karen for her wonderful Foreword. And to Gillian for her Introduction.

I am grateful also to my book designer and illustrator – Peggy Sands – whom I have had the pleasure of working with for the first time, and who not only provided me with professional but also personal advice on this long journey toward publication.

Finally, to my family, a big and warm thank-you. To Paul, who supported me in every way possible – I love you. To my son, Tim, whose tireless editing, and aesthetic advice has only helped make this book better in so many ways.

And to my giver of bear hugs – Jonathan – without whom, this book would not exist.

Thank you all so much, for your love, inspiration, and patience.

Theresa Fuller
Sydney 7th of December 2022

Thank You

Thank you for reading my book, I hope you enjoyed it and found it helpful! If so, please consider leaving a review on my Amazon page. This helps others who are considering purchasing the book, and supports me to continue writing.

To review, scan the barcode below or go to
https://www.amazon.com/stores/Theresa-Fuller/author/B07B6HF1XS.

Theresa Fuller
theresafuller.com

www.ingramcontent.com/pod-product-compliance
Lightning Source LLC
Chambersburg PA
CBHW042106090526

44590CB00004B/112